WHERE PEOPLE LIVE

LIFE IN A TOWN

WRITTEN BY
Robin Twiddy

KidHaven PUBLISHING

Published in 2025 by
KidHaven Publishing, an Imprint of
Greenhaven Publishing, LLC
2544 Clinton St., Buffalo, NY 14224

Written by: Robin Twiddy
Edited by: Rebecca Phillips-Bartlett
Designed by: Jasmine Pointer

Cataloging-in-Publication Data

Names: Twiddy, Robin.
Title: Life in a town / Robin Twiddy.
Description: Buffalo, NY : KidHaven Publishing, 2025. | Series: Where people live | Includes glossary and index.
Identifiers: ISBN 9781534549135 (pbk.) | ISBN 9781534549142 (library bound) | ISBN 9781534549159 (ebook)
Subjects: LCSH: Cities and towns--Juvenile literature.
Classification: LCC HT119.T88 2025 | DDC 307.76--dc23

Manufactured in the United States of America

CPSIA compliance information: Batch #CW25KH
For further information contact Greenhaven Publishing LLC at 1-844-317-7404.

Please visit our website, www.greenhavenpublishing.com.
For a free color catalog of all our high-quality books, call toll free 1-844-317-7404 or fax 1-844-317-7405.

Find us on

IMAGE CREDITS

All images are courtesy of Shutterstock.com. With thanks to Getty Images, Thinkstock Photo and iStockphoto.
Cover – HappyPictures, Picksell, PIYATHILAKA, Mihai_Andritoiu. Alien Character – HappyPictures. Background throughout – Picksell. 4–5 – NicoElNino, Kosoff, Wangkun Jia, maxrob27. 6–7 – IR Stone, Sean Pavone. 8–9 – Margaret.Wiktor, Wileydoc. 10–11 – Stuart Monk, Sean Pavone, OJUP, James R. Martin, Jason Finn, Andriy Blokhin, digidreamgrafix. 12–13 – Amorn Suriyan, kornnphoto. 14–15 – doublelee, Arina P Habich. 16–17 – Joseph Sohm, Monkey Business Images. 18–19 – Inside Creative House, Drazen Zigic. 20–21 – MathieuLphoto, Jon Chica. 22–23 – Leigh Trail, 19 STUDIO.

CONTENTS

WORDS THAT LOOK LIKE THIS CAN BE FOUND IN THE GLOSSARY ON PAGE 24.

WELCOME TO EARTH

Hello, my fellow Morpians. My name is Morp. Thank you for tuning in to another episode of *Where People Live* – the show where we explore Earth and the humans living there to learn about where humans live.

Humans live almost everywhere on Earth. From hot to cold places, from wet to dry places, humans have made **SETTLEMENTS** all over the world. Today we will be looking at towns.

WHAT HUMANS MEAN

SETTLEMENTS: Anywhere that a group of people builds a place to live

WHAT ON EARTH IS A TOWN?

There are lots of people living here in the town - more than in most villages, but not as many as in a city. So, what is a town?

A town is a RESIDENTIAL area. Towns can be big, small, or somewhere in between.

Towns can have very different **POPULATIONS**. Some towns only have 1,000 people living there, while others can have many thousands. In the U.S., different states have different rules about what makes a place a town.

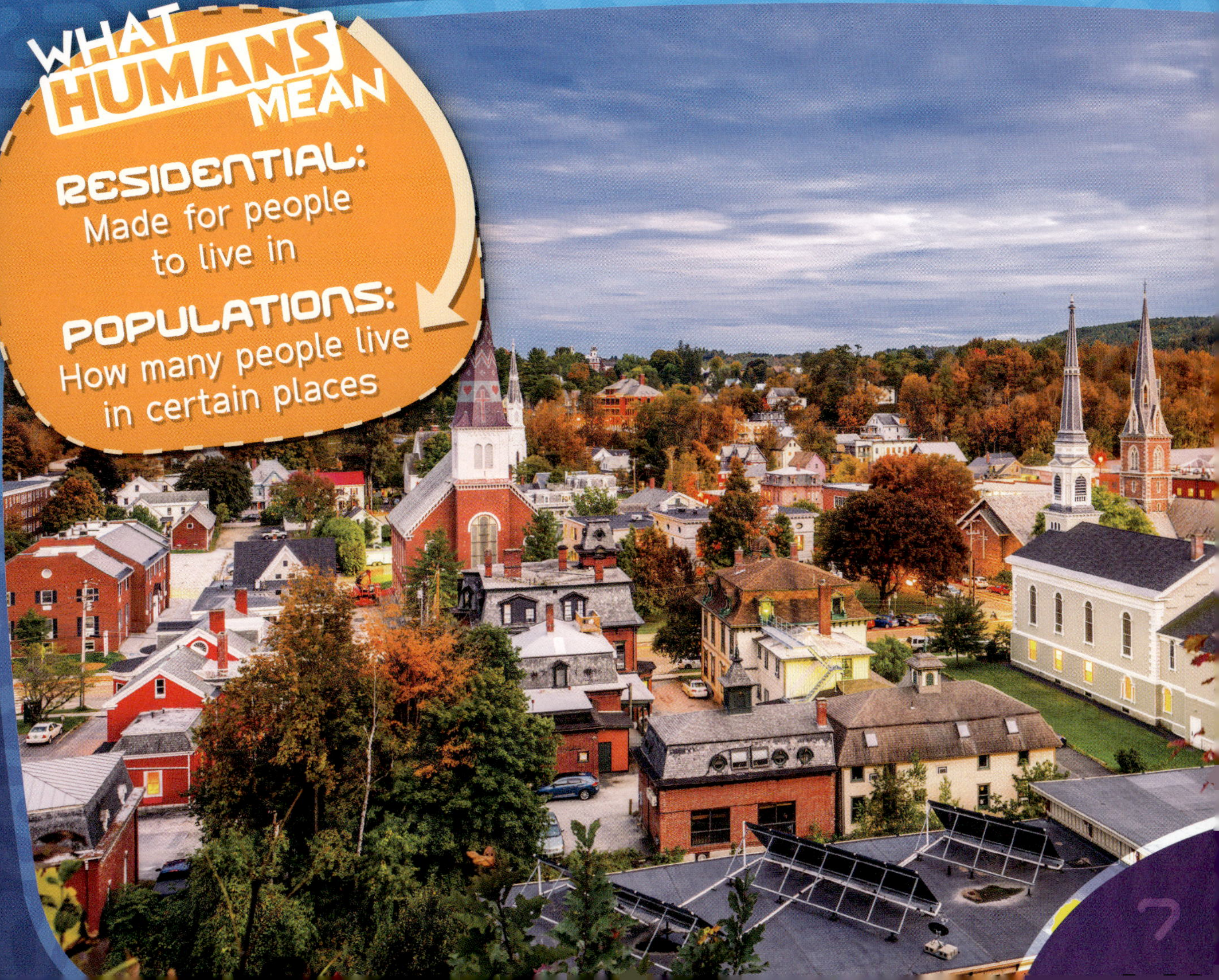

WHAT HUMANS MEAN

RESIDENTIAL: Made for people to live in

POPULATIONS: How many people live in certain places

WHERE ARE THEY GOING?

Most of the people running around this town live here. Towns are often built around a type of INDUSTRY. People may come from outside the town to work in that industry.

With this many people visiting and living in a town, it needs to have lots of FACILITIES. All these people need to eat, sleep, exercise, play, learn, and do all the other amazing things that humans do.

WHAT HUMANS MEAN

INDUSTRY: The people, places, and work involved in making money

FACILITIES: Places, buildings, and equipment needed for certain activities

WHAT IS IN A TOWN?

Well, after following a few of the humans around, I saw a lot of interesting things in the town. Here are some of the places I saw.

TOWN HALL

SHOPS AND OTHER BUSINESSES

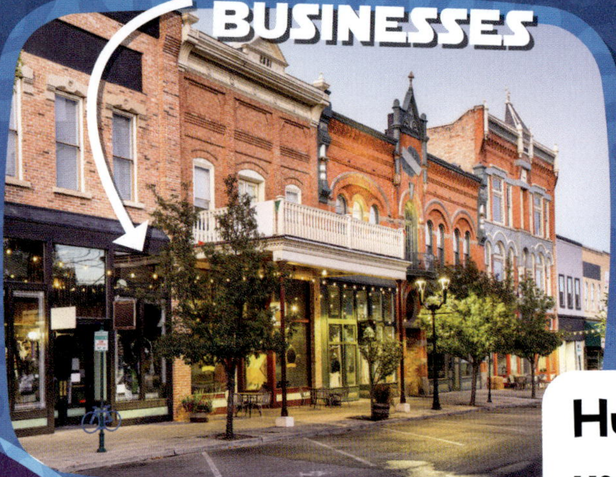

PLACES OF WORSHIP

Humans who belong to a **religion** use these places to **pray** and **worship**.

FACTORIES

BUS AND TRAIN STATIONS

Buses and train stations connect towns to other places humans want to go to.

HOUSES... LOTS OF HOUSES

SCHOOLS

HAVING FUN IN THE TOWN

Humans like to have fun. With so many people living in the same area, towns need facilities for people to enjoy themselves. Parks are **GREEN SPACES** in towns.

WHAT HUMANS MEAN

GREEN SPACES: Places in built-up areas with trees, grass, and other natural things

Humans like to walk, play, and exercise in parks. This human is having fun swinging!

Towns often have sports or RECREATION centers where people can go to keep fit and have fun.

WHAT HUMANS MEAN

RECREATION: Activities to do with relaxing and having fun

SOME HUMANS SEEM TO GO SHOPPING FOR FUN TOO.

SHOPPING IN THE TOWN

Towns usually have more stores than villages, but fewer than cities. Stores have everything that the humans who live there need. Stores also provide jobs for the people who live there.

A town might have a market. Markets often sell fresh food and things made LOCALLY. Some markets are open all the time. Some only open on certain days.

WHAT HUMANS MEAN

LOCALLY: To do with a particular small area, such as a town

SOME TOWNS HAVE FARMERS' MARKETS WHERE LOCAL FARMERS CAN SELL WHAT THEY HAVE GROWN.

TOWN HALLS

Town halls are an important part of a town. This is where decisions about how the town is run are made. People who live in the **community** can sometimes come to meetings at town halls.

WHAT HUMANS MEAN

COMMUNITY: To do with a group of people who have something in common, such as where they live

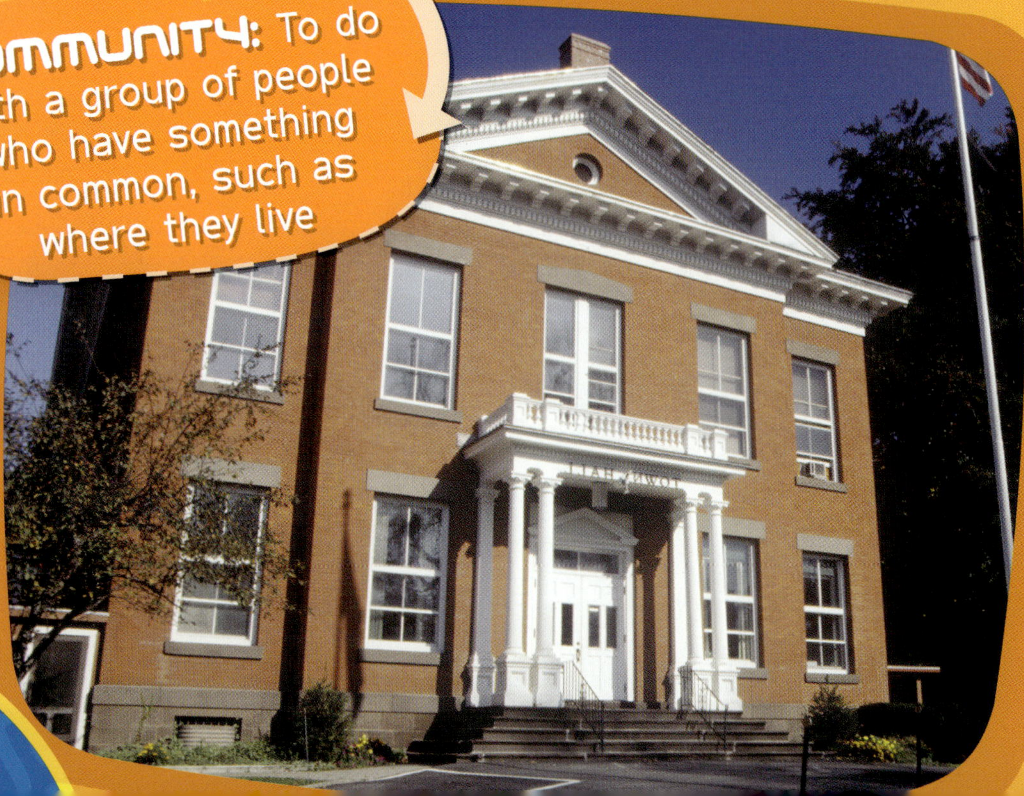

Town hall meetings give the people in the community an **opportunity** to discuss what is happening in their town. They can talk to the people who make decisions.

SCHOOLS

Oh look! Those children are all getting on the same yellow bus. I wonder where they are going.

They are going to school. A large town will usually have more than one school.

There are schools for humans of all different ages. There are even schools for adults who want to keep learning. More education can help humans get new jobs in their town.

BUSINESSES IN THE TOWN

Towns do not just have places to learn, have fun, and buy things. They also have businesses. Businesses give people in the town jobs and bring money in from outside the town.

Settlements that grow into towns often start because of an ECONOMIC opportunity. This might be AGRICULTURE, fishing, manufacturing, or mining. This is often based on where the town is.

WHAT HUMANS MEAN

ECONOMIC: To do with business and money

AGRICULTURE: To do with farming

THIS TOWN HAS GROWN AROUND A FISHING OPPORTUNITY.

TUNE in NEXT WEEK

Well, viewers, human towns are very interesting. They are very busy, with lots of things happening in them. Since there are many people, towns need lots of facilities for the people who live there.

Whether you live in a village, town, or a city, they are all connected by roads, rivers, and railways. A town looks like a lovely place to live... if you are a human!

GLOSSARY

MANUFACTURING making a material or materials into something with use or value, often to be sold

MINING digging in the ground for valuable materials

NATURAL found in nature and not made by people

OPPORTUNITY a chance to do something

PRAY to talk to a god or gods of a chosen belief

RELIGION an organized set of beliefs usually centered around a god or gods

WORSHIP a religious act where a person expresses praise for a god or gods

INDEX